Honest Money

By

Carl Martin Andersen

Published by Valkyrie Resources, LLC

Print: 978-0-9911456-0-7

Kindle: 978-0-9911456-1-4

Dedication

This book is dedicated to Ludwig Heinrich Edler von Mises, a prominent force behind the Austrian School of Economics, which advocates a responsible monetary policy wherein money has stable and intrinsic value.

> *His most eminent qualities were his inflexible honesty, his unhesitating sincerity. He never yielded. He always freely enunciated what he considered to be true. If he had been prepared to suppress or only to soften his criticisms of popular, but irresponsible, policies, the most influential positions and offices would have been offered him. But he never compromised.*

> —Margit Herzfeld Serény, widow of Ludwig Von Mises

It has been said that integrity is a state of being where one's actions match one's stated beliefs.

By that definition, Professor Doctor Von Mises set an example we all, especially our political leaders, should strive to emulate.

Forethought

The Bank of the United States is one of the most deadly hostilities existing, against the principles and form of our Constitution. An institution like this, penetrating by its branches every part of the Union, acting by command and in phalanx, may, in a critical moment, upset the government. I deem no government safe which is under the vassalage of any self-constituted authorities, or any other authority than that of the nation, or its regular functionaries. What an obstruction could not this bank of the United States, with all its branch banks, be in time of war! It might dictate to us the peace we should accept, or withdraw its aids. Ought we then to give further growth to an institution so powerful, so hostile?

—Thomas Jefferson to Albert Gallatin, 1803

To put the above quote in a modern perspective, the reader should simply replace "The Bank of the United States" with "The Federal Reserve System."

Preface

In the course of conversations with hundreds of people, both in person and on Internet forums, I am often asked, "If not paper dollars, then what?"

The answer, of course, is money that has intrinsic value such as silver and gold.

Many people don't understand why the latter is better than the former.

Those who do understand often wonder, "How do I buy precious metals?" And perhaps more importantly, "How will I spend them?"

Others wisely note that if we expect our economic system to eventually collapse, gold and silver by themselves won't keep our families alive. They ask, "How can we prepare?"

This short treatise is intended to help answer those questions.

Chapter 1

A Short History of Money and Banking

Money is a mysterious subject for most people. It's just "out there," and we can go earn it if we work for it. Most people would say that the vast majority of their personal problems stem from not having enough money.

There is little understanding of exactly where money comes from and how the money supply affects the economy. The truth is, the basic foundation of the information we're taught in public schools and universities is based on a big lie.

Before we get into that, we need to have a solid understanding of one economic concept: **the Law of Supply and Demand**

The Law of Supply and Demand

Most of us have been taught the basics of supply and demand. It's easy to understand that if there is a large supply of a particular product available, simple competition will cause the market price of that product to drop. Conversely, if there is a shortage of a specific, in-demand product, then the price of that product will naturally rise.

When I was in high school, a popular urban legend among car lovers was the story of the 1959 Chevy Corvette somebody bought for a song. After its owner was killed fighting in Vietnam, it just sat in the garage and finally, after 10 years, his mother advertised it for sale as an "old Chevrolet" and sold it for $50. Wow, what a profit for the buyer! It was worth thousands!

We can all intuitively understand why such a rare and special car demands a high price, but imagine this: if every soldier killed in Vietnam (over 58,000) had stashed a similar Corvette in his parents' garage, and on the same day in 1980, all those parents, realizing the current street price of the car, had decided to sell. Also imagine that they were all "eager" to sell and had advertised their son's car for sale for $10,000. In 1980 (not the happiest of economic times), would there really have been more than 50,000 people each ready buy one of those Corvettes for $10,000 in cash?

You might say, "Well, if they waited long enough!" That's true, but buyers and sellers don't generally wait if they are ready to make a deal. Some of the sellers would be willing to negotiate, and, naturally, those willing to negotiate the most would sell their car the fastest. This would have the effect of driving down the street price of all similar Corvettes, including those that were already owned by other collectors and enthusiasts.

Imagine Thanksgiving in America in a year where 90% of the turkeys in the USA died of (the imaginary disease) "Turkey Flu," causing an extreme shortage. Do you think the farmers and the supermarkets that owned the remaining frozen turkeys could, during the high-demand holiday season, set a higher price for them?

Do you think they would, especially given the lost opportunity to sell all the turkeys that died of the flu?

Only the naïve would think they wouldn't.

That is the law of supply and demand at work. The reason the review was necessary is that it's key to the statement I'm about to make.

Money is a commodity.

It's really no different than turkeys, Corvettes, wheat, corn, gold, or silver.

This is the most important point in the book, so it bears repeating:

Money is a commodity. Call it a "product" if you like; that is quite accurate. Money is not just controlled by banks. Banks are not just people smart enough to have a lot of money. Banks are *manufacturers* of money.

Banks are factories.

Their product is money.

We were all taught about the law of supply and demand

and how it applies to the price of commodities and consumer products, but what we were *not* taught is that the same law applies to that commodity known as "money." We weren't taught this because the bankers don't want us to know it.

If we understand that money is a commodity no different than any other commodity, then we begin to understand the scam that has been perpetrated on us.

This is not a new subject. It has been around since the Roman Empire, if not earlier. Ever wonder why dimes and quarters have little grooves (known as "reeding") cut around the edge instead of being smooth like nickels and pennies? It's to prevent what's known as "coin clipping," a practice started, at least officially, by the Roman government.

Coin clipping is where a little bit of the edge of the coin is "clipped" or filed off. Clip off and save enough little pieces, and you eventually have enough metal to make another coin.

Coin clipping was a sort of secret "tax" that was not generally perceptible to the people. It's an excellent example of inflation because it's easy to see how the number of coins increased without actually increasing the amount of gold in circulation.

Quarters and dimes produced in the USA prior to 1965 were made of 90% silver. The reeding on the rim was to prevent modern-day coin clipping by making it more obvious that metal had gone missing.

So, getting back to our discussion of supply and demand, imagine this: What if 80% of the money in the US economy simply disappeared? That means 100% of us would be out there competing to earn the remaining 20%. Clearly, either 80% of us are going to be completely disappointed, or most of us are going to have to be satisfied with a lot less than we're accustomed.

What would that do to the price of labor? There are already a lot of workers out there competing to earn money from a pool that has become very small. Is it possible that some workers would be willing to discount their work just to ensure they have a job? (A number of experiences in the airline industry convinced me that they would.) Do you suppose employers might further reduce wages? The supply of labor would be large, and the demand (represented by the amount of money available to pay for it) would be small.

Of course the price of labor would drop. Conversely, what if the money supply suddenly increased fivefold? There would be a lot of money out there for a relatively small pool of labor. Would the workers flock to those companies paying the highest wages? Of course they would!

This would drive the price of labor up, right? Whether it's commodities or labor, increasing the amount of money in circulation by a given percentage will eventually cause the prices to increase by the same percentage. In other words, if we double the money supply, prices will eventually double. We have decreased the "price" of money by increasing the supply, stealing a little bit of value from the existing money each time we add to the amount in circulation.

It's important not to confuse "price" with "value." The price of a given commodity (such as eggs) is only a reflection of its value expressed in a quantity of another commodity (money). If a market price changes, it's usually because the money changes value, not the eggs.

Now that we understand how supply and demand works, let's look at the history of banking.

The First Banker

Back in the Middle Ages, they didn't have banks. People either carried their money with them or else hid it in their houses. Some people who wanted more security for their personal wealth sought out a safe place to keep it, but the only people who had vaults or safes were goldsmiths because they naturally had a supply of gold and needed to keep it safe from robbers and thieves.

Goldsmiths started storing other people's gold for a fee. People would pay them a certain amount per month or year for storing their gold in the vault. The goldsmith would issue a paper receipt, stamped with his personal seal, for the specific items or amount of gold on deposit with him. This was the first use of what became known in the bullion business as a "warehouse receipt."

When people wanted to spend their gold, they would take the warehouse receipt to the goldsmith, claim their gold, and hand their coins over in exchange for their purchase or to complete their business transaction. Eventually, it became more convenient to just hand over the receipt to the merchant instead, the buyer perhaps signing his or her name to it transferring ownership to the merchant. This saved a lot of time and effort since people didn't have to go to the goldsmith to spend their gold.

As this practice grew, certain goldsmiths became well-known and earned reputations for being trustworthy. Their warehouse receipts were recognized and more easily exchanged (spent). It became commonplace to exchange these warehouse receipts for other commodities, while the gold itself remained safe in the goldsmiths' vaults.

On a fateful day for humanity, one of these enterprising goldsmiths (whose name is lost to history, but I'm guessing it was "Warburg.") woke up in the middle of the night and realized that he had so much gold on deposit and so many warehouse receipts in circulation that nobody except him knew exactly how much there was. At the same moment he realized that it was very unlikely all his customers were going to come to his shop and demand their gold at the same time, so if he were to make up a receipt for gold that he didn't have—*gold that did not exist*—nobody would know!

With that idea fresh in his mind, he got out of bed, went to his desk, and made up a nice new warehouse receipt for gold that he didn't have. After a nutritious breakfast, he went down to the local Chevrolet Dealership and traded that (fake) warehouse receipt for a brand-new split-window Corvette Convertible in candy apple red.

OK, maybe it was a horse and buggy or a piece of land or something, but you get the idea.

And that, ladies and gentlemen, is the first instance of the use of what John Maynard Keynes came to call "fractional reserve banking." In other words, the goldsmith only had a fraction of the gold in his vault for which he had issued receipts. No one knew how much gold he had in his vault except him.

Since he had liberally loaned his made-up warehouse receipts to his king, the king was unwilling to audit the goldsmith's vault to prove that everyone's gold was actually there, despite the many "Audit the Goldsmith" campaigns instigated by his customers.

Flashing forward well into the future, we have a very similar system. We use what are known as "Federal Reserve Notes" (FRNs), which are issued by the Federal Reserve Bank. They have no intrinsic value, they are decidedly *not* backed by gold or silver, and (most importantly) **the Federal Reserve Bank is not part of the US Government**.

Oh yes, they play great theater in having the President of the United States appoint and the Senate confirm the appointment of the "Chairman of the Board of Governors of the Federal Reserve System" (Wow! Doesn't that sound official?) so they can pretend it's a government agency, but it is not.

The Federal Reserve is a privately owned bank, and you would be surprised to learn who the actual owners are. Do your own due diligence (DYODD) and research if you're interested.

If you don't believe that the Fed is privately-owned, look up the phone number of any of the regional Federal Reserve Banks, call them, and ask the receptionist, "Is the

Federal Reserve System a government agency?" They do a lot of pretending and insinuating on the public stage, but if you ask them directly, they will tell you the truth.

What's truly amazing is that this doesn't seem to bother most people, even when they begin to understand it. I refer the reader back to the quote from Henry Ford: "It is well enough that people of the nation do not understand our banking and monetary system, for if they did, I believe there would be a revolution before tomorrow morning."

Chapter 2

Central Banking

To understand how central banking works—and why it's so dangerous—let's take a look at the explanation contained in my book *Once Upon a Time*. While this is a very simplistic model for a concept often described by banks in very confusing technical terminology known as "Greenspeak" (named after the incomprehensible gobbledygook that spewed from the mouth of Alan Greenspan, former Fed Chairman, when he testified before Congress), a serious investigation by the reader will show there is no factual error.

It works something like this: Say you had an island with five farms on it and you decided to give those farms to five different people who agreed to live there forever. The only rule is that you get to be the banker and print all the money (and they don't get to bring any with them). Before these five new farmers can buy tools or even eggs from each other, they need to get some money from you. You agree to loan each farmer $100 for one year at ten percent interest. That means that in one year, each farmer will have to pay you $110. They promise that they will pay you the $110 or give you their farm.

Let's see how this would work: You loan $100 to each farmer, so there is a total of $500 circulating in our little "economy." The farmers grow their crops and raise their animals and buy and sell to each other for a year. Then the day comes they must all pay up. The first farmer pays you $110 and thanks you for the loan. Since you, the banker, now have $110 of the original $500 that was in circulation, there is only $390 left in circulation. The second farmer pays you $110 and thanks you for the loan. There is now $280 left in circulation.

Do you notice how, as the farmers pay the banker, the amount of money in circulation is reduced?

The third farmer pays you $110 and thanks you for the loan. Now there is $170 left in circulation. The fourth farmer pays you the $110 he owes you, leaving $60 in circulation.

The last farmer approaches you with a long face. He says that he doesn't have enough money to pay you back. He explains he had a hard year, and even though his friends, the other four farmers, loaned him all the money they had to help him pay, he still only has $60. You make a sympathetic face, but you smile inside because you know that *there never was enough money for him to pay.* You tell him you're sorry but remind him of your agreement.

At this point you, the banker, have a choice. You have the authority to take his farm away from him right then and there. Because you're a smart banker, though, you offer the fifth farmer another loan (plus you don't like actually working, especially on a farm). You know that farmers work a lot harder if they *think* they own the farm. Of course he has to borrow enough to pay off the old loan, plus some extra to live on. It gives him a chance to keep his farm, so naturally he takes it.

The other farmers also have to borrow some money so they can operate their businesses and live their lives as well—remember, when they paid back their loans, all the money in our little economy went back into the bank. And again, the money they borrow is never (and will never be) enough to pay back all the loans plus interest, so at least one of them will have the same problem next year as farmer number five did this year.

You, the banker, will probably just keep loaning money back to them so you can keep them working for you on their farms, earning the money to pay you interest. But whenever you want, you can just reduce the money supply (by not loaning out any more) so the loans can't be repaid and you can start taking their farms away from them.

Smart central bankers have learned over the years that they can control almost anything by increasing or decreasing the amount of money in circulation. By increasing the amount of money they are willing to loan, the bankers can simulate prosperity and a growing economy.

They can trick people like farmers and other people into borrowing money at low interest. The people who borrow the money use it to improve their farms, build houses, or open other businesses which have actual value.

Whenever they want to, the bankers can reduce the amount of money they lend. Less money then goes into circulation, and as people continue to make their loan payments, the pool of money shrinks even more. There is less and less money out there for people to earn.

Since it becomes harder and harder to earn money, more and more people are unable to make their loan payments and the banks seize their houses, buildings, farms, and businesses.

Essentially, the banks use easy loans as bait to get people to work for them. Whenever they wish, they can stop lending money, which causes the money supply to dry up. When that happens, all the assets in the economy are easy pickings, and they have the government courts and law-enforcement people to help them take peoples' property.

See why it's so dangerous to put bankers in charge of the money?

Carrying our little island story farther, let's say that you, the banker, like many bankers before you, decide that you'd like to have a nice bank building to work in. (Bankers dwell in marble halls...) It's such an arduous job administering all those loans, and you feel you could be more efficient in a more comfortable space.

Will you borrow money from the farmers to build it?

Hell no!

You just fire up your little printing machine and print yourself $500. Now assuming this is the first year of the island adventure, when you pay the farmers $500 for the labor and materials to build the bank building, it will go into circulation with the other $500. This effectively doubles the amount of money in circulation making the total $1000. (M1, for you economists).

We know from our earlier discussion of supply and demand that doubling the money supply will eventually cause the prices of other commodities (in comparison to the money) to double as well. If eggs were a dollar a dozen before the increase, they would eventually be two dollars a dozen because there would be double the amount of dollars out there competing to buy the same number of eggs.

Entrepreneurial readers, especially fans of the movie *Trading Places*, will say, "Yeah but if you invested in eggs before the increase in the money supply, you could double your money!"

Let's examine that further. Say you, the banker, quietly tell one of the farmers (John) that you're going to double the money supply by buying the bank building, which will cause all prices to double. Farmer John takes that information and secretly buys ten dozen eggs for ten dollars and stores them in his refrigerator.

You build the building, pay the farmers, and inflation causes the expected rise in prices of all commodities traded on the island. Farmer John sells his ten dozen eggs for two dollars a dozen and jumps for joy, saying, "I doubled my money!"

Think about this.

What can Farmer John now buy with that $20 dollars? Well, keeping the conversation simple, let's make it eggs. Can he buy double the amount of eggs he could before?

Nope. He can still only buy ten dozen eggs. And remember, the price of other commodities will have doubled as well.

What doubled beside the money supply?

Nothing.

Did he make a profit?

Nope.

Was it a smart move to buy eggs?

Yes, because it preserved his buying power, but he only preserved the ability to buy the same amount of eggs or other commodities that he could before. There was no profit for anyone except the banker. Farmer John converted an asset with an unstable value (money) into an asset with a stable value (eggs). The price of the eggs went up but the value did not; in other words, the value of the eggs remained the same, but *the value of the money was cut in half.*

Inflation is not the rising prices of commodities. Inflation is the increasing volume of dollars in circulation, which causes the value of each individual dollar to shrink. It is important to remember that "price" is not the same as "value." Value seldom changes much.

It is said that a Roman could buy a custom-made toga, a belt, and a pair of shoes for one ounce of gold. Today, a good quality, made-to-measure suit, shoes, belt, and maybe a shirt can be bought for, you guessed it, about an ounce of gold.

Now, with all that in mind, ask yourself this: Who *actually* paid for the new bank building on our fantasy island?

If you can wrap your mind around that last question, you will begin to understand why G. Edward Griffin calls inflation an "invisible tax."

Chapter 3

Three Kinds of Paper Money

There are three kinds of paper "money" circulating in the USA besides the actual gold and silver coins required by our Constitution. These three types of money are not the same! Indeed they are very, very different in where they come from (i.e. who produces them) and how they affect inflation.

In order, from worst to best, they are:

Federal Reserve Notes

United States Notes

Silver Certificates

Of these three, the first two are a type of "money" known as fiat money. "Fiat" means "order or decree," so "fiat money" is money that has value by order or decree. Ever take a look at a Federal Reserve note where it says, "This note is legal tender for all debts, public and private"? In other words, you must accept FRNs as payment of a debt. If you refuse, the debt is considered discharged, and the debtor's obligation cancelled. This is an order, or "fiat," from your government to accept this form of money to settle any debts.

Imagine that you lived back when gold and silver were more commonly used as money and you had loaned a friend $10 in gold. The bankers want you to accept their paper money (remember the goldsmith's new Corvette?), so they use the power of the government to force you to accept a paper $10 bill instead of the $10 in gold. Under the legal tender laws, if your friend attempts to pay you in paper money (Federal Reserve Notes) and you refuse because you want the gold you loaned him in the first place, your friend's debt to you is considered discharged and he doesn't have to pay you anything anymore!

When the government and banking cabal does something

like this, it's called "banking regulation," but when organized crime does it, it's called "extortion."

Today, Silver Certificates and United States Notes are very rarely seen in circulation, having been replaced by the ubiquitous Federal Reserve Notes.

Federal Reserve Notes

Image courtesy of Jimmy Haagenson

Federal Reserve Notes are issued (manufactured) by the Federal Reserve Banks that make up the Federal Reserve System. The Federal Reserve Banks and their affiliate banks also have the authority to create "digital" FRNs that are not actually ever printed. These are the dollars electronically transferred back and forth between banks. They "spend" just like paper dollars and they contribute to inflation in exactly the same way, so except for the printing on paper, they are exactly the same as paper FRNs. Henceforth, we'll use the term "FRN" to refer to both.

FRNs only come into existence, or circulation, when someone borrows them. The Fed creates dollars to loan to the Federal Government, and your local bank creates dollars for your car loan, credit card, mortgage, etc. It's all the same even though the actual physical printing may take place somewhere else.

The story we were told as children that the bank uses money in people's savings accounts to make loans to other people is a *barefaced lie.*

Federal Reserve Notes contribute to inflation and, for the government (i.e. the people), they represent a debt that must be repaid. When you see a figure for however many squillions of dollars the US national debt is, remember that every single one of them, except for the accrued interest, came into existence when the government borrowed it.

United States Notes

Image courtesy of Jimmy Haagenson

United States Notes (USNs) are also fiat money, but they are issued (manufactured under the authority of) directly by the United States Treasury. They are not borrowed and there is no debt attached to them. The treasury prints them and the government spends them, putting them in circulation.

When Abraham Lincoln didn't want to deal with central bankers during the War Between the States, his administration issued United States Notes (dollars) printed in distinctive green ink. The green color distinguished them from the bank-issued dollars, and they came to be known as "greenbacks," a moniker that is still used as a nickname for all US Dollars.

The only United States Notes issued in my lifetime were printed in 1963 under the orders of President John F. Kennedy. Readers may draw their own conclusions about the coincidence of two of our most revered presidents, who defied the central bankers and issued dollars directly from the US Treasury, who were then assassinated.

US Notes are fiat money and do contribute to inflation, but they do not have any debt attached to them. Besides the nominal cost of printing, there is no further obligation attached to them. They do *not* make the national debt grow.

www.ingramcontent.com/pod-product-compliance
Lightning Source LLC
Chambersburg PA
CBHW070947210326
41520CB00021B/7089

Silver Certificates

Image courtesy of Jimmy Haagenson

Silver Certificates are warehouse receipts for actual silver dollar coins held in treasury vaults. They are simply a more convenient way to carry money, much like the warehouse receipts from the goldsmith we discussed earlier. Unlike the other "notes" (a note, i.e. "promissory note," is an instrument of debt.), this certificate is payable in demand by actual silver dollars. Silver Certificates, when properly administered, are not inflationary and do not have any debt attached to them.

As banks and even the US Treasury commonly do with silver and gold-backed certificates, they issued more paper than they had silver to back it up with, so eventually they created a policy to stop exchanging them for silver dollars.

Why would they stop redeeming perfectly valid warehouse receipts? Payable "on demand" to the "bearer" in silver? Their explanation is that some of the dollars had more collector value than others, so to be fair to everyone, they stopped exchanging them. (I am not making this up! DYODD if you doubt it).

Knowing what you know now, do you buy this story?

Final Thoughts on Fiat Money
and US Central Banking

We've learned what inflation is and what causes it.

We've learned about fiat money and the two main types used in the United States.

So in case it isn't obvious, here's a question I think we should all be asking ourselves:

"If the US Treasury can create fiat money on its own, why do we give a license to the Federal Reserve to print fiat money, which we then borrow and have to pay back with interest?"

If you understand this question, then you are probably beginning to understand why more and more people are clamoring to pass the "Audit the Fed" bill.

I will end this chapter with a quote from Congressman Charles August Lindbergh, Sr., who was the father of the famous transatlantic pilot. Congressman Lindbergh made the following statement on the floor of the United States House of Representatives on December 23rd, 1913, expressing his opposition to the "Federal Reserve Act."

> *This [Federal Reserve Act] establishes the most gigantic trust on earth. When the President (Woodrow Wilson) signs this bill, the invisible government of the monetary power will be legalized….the worst legislative crime of the ages is perpetrated by this banking and currency bill.*

…the worst legislative crime of the ages…

Chapter 4

If Not Fiat Money, Then What?

If it's not obvious by now, your humble author is an advocate of *honest money*, which is to say money with intrinsic value. Silver and gold have proven, since the dawn of time, to be the most stable and universally accepted forms of money. There are all sorts of arguments made by statists and bankers as to why silver and gold backed money won't work, but the really amusing one is "There's just not enough!"

Well of course there's not enough! Fiat money can be issued in amounts leading to infinity, but the silver and gold on this planet exist in limited amounts. That's both why they are considered valuable *and* why they make such a stable platform on which to base an economic system.

The supply of precious metals, in an honest system, naturally sets limitations on the amount of money a government can spend because they cannot invisibly tax the people with inflation and spend money that never existed.

We've talked about chickens and eggs ad nauseum (unless you like omelets, which I do), so let's take it a step further and talk about chicken farmers. We'll start with the postulate that the amount of energy, effort, and chicken feed required to produce an egg hasn't changed since the first chick hatched and asked his Mommy, "Which one of us came first?" Nowadays, chicken farms are highly scientific and automated operations. Very little human exertion is required except to supervise and oversee.

Why did the farmers buy all this expensive equipment? Is it because they just like technology and "need" the newest version like my son needs the newest iPod? Or did they buy this stuff because they thought it would make them more efficient? Did they think they would make more profit by increasing efficiency?

The technology of chicken farming has advanced geometrically even in my lifetime. To say that these outfits are at the peak of efficiency is an understatement. Now, continuing with another postulate that competition remains fairly constant, wouldn't greater efficiency result in a drop in the sale price of eggs? That's exactly what would happen in a stable economy where money has a standard and intrinsic value. Efficiency increases over time with the advancement of technology, which translates into lower prices and an improved standard of living for everyone.

If the reader feels like I've been overdoing the "Inflation Bad" theme, I'm glad you've noticed.

So here's the answer to the question, "If not fiat money, then what?" Obviously it's gold and silver money.

From a broader perspective, and with a look into the very real potential for a US and world economic collapse even worse than the Great Depression of the 1930s, readers might be asking, "What can I do?"

- Get out of debt.
- Put at least some of your savings into gold and silver bullion that stays in your possession.
- Put some of your savings into food and supplies in case of natural or man-made disaster.

Everyone must do their own due diligence and determine the amount of change in their lifestyle and the depth of preparation they require. DYODD—Do Your Own Due Diligence—should be a watchword. Do not believe the hype, *especially* the hype on television. Learn the facts for yourself; this short paper is just a primer. There are so many things to learn, and an unknown amount of time to prepare.

Getting Out of Debt

Get out of debt as soon as you can. If that means giving up some of the things you enjoy, then do it. If it means putting off that new car, then do it.

Create a plan, automate it to the extent possible (like with automatic payments from your bank), and then stick to it. If you need help, there are hundreds of organizations, charities, religious groups, commercial companies, and government agencies to help you. Google "debt help" and take your pick. Be sure you understand how any deal you make with a creditor will affect your credit score. Do your own due diligence, know and understand the deals you make, if any—but any way you can, clear that debt balance.

The economy may not collapse suddenly as it did in 1929. It may just slowly contract. What that means is that while the numbers in your credit card debt will remain the same (or, more than likely, grow), the amount of dollars you earn will grow much less quickly or actually drop. Whether it's just by increasing taxes or whether your salary goes down (or you simply lose your job), you can pretty much count on having less money to spend.

In my mind, the exception to this rule is your mortgage. As the economy collapses, the number of dollars you owe on your mortgage will be unaffected. If you keep a good amount of your savings in gold and silver, inflation (maybe even hyperinflation) will ensure that its price increases, probably more rapidly than other commodities, and that reserve could be used to make your payments or even pay off your mortgage at some point.

This plan is only viable and safe if you actually have the discipline to invest in gold and silver—and leave the investment alone (i.e. don't sell gold to buy a new fishing boat).

If I were in a position right now to pay off my mortgage, I'd use the money to buy gold and silver instead, wait until inflation increases the price of the gold and silver several times (it will), and use a portion of it to pay off the mortgage.

Gold and Silver Bullion

The first thing to understand is Ponce' Law:

"If you don't hold it, you don't own it."

This is a warning against paper silver and gold in the form of certificates or pooled accounts. The amount of paper silver and gold certificates on this planet for which the actual, physical silver and gold does not exist is many multiples of the actual metals available. The specifics are beyond the scope of this paper, but understand it is critical to have it in your possession because eventually everyone will want to actually hold their metals.

Ever play musical chairs as a kid?

Did the other kids ever help you get a chair when the music stopped?

Think about it.

Don't rely on safe deposit boxes. During the Great Depression, depositors were not allowed to open their safe deposit boxes unless they were in the presence of an IRS agent. Don't think the government would do that again? In the market for a bridge?

Do not accept certificates of any kind. The actual physical metal should be in your hands and in a place you always control. Storing precious metals is an art and science by itself. Check out http://goldismoney2.com for hundreds of pages of discussion on the matter. It's a good source for general metals investment information as well.

My philosophy on which precious metals to buy assumes an economic collapse so severe that paper dollars are either nearly worthless due to inflation or not accepted at all. The people who have the things I need—food, drink, fuel, medical supplies, etc.—will want to trade for something with intrinsic value. That may be in the form of bartered supplies, or it may be gold or silver.

For this reason, I want my silver and gold to be "fungible" (i.e. easily broken up into small denominations) so the seller doesn't have to "make change" with silver he or she may not have.

I also want it easily identifiable by an average person. For this reason, I start my silver accumulation with 1964 and earlier US dimes and quarters. These are made from 90% silver, and I reckon that in an economic collapse every trader will recognize these familiar coins and understand their silver content. This type of silver is known as "junk" silver, which is to say that the silver value in the coins is greater than the collector value.

A quick comment about collectibles and rare coins: They are decidedly not insurance for the future. Their price at any given time depends on a prosperous, growing economy. When people have a lot of FRNs, the price of collectible coins goes up, but during economic troubled times, the prices drop.

I have bought a lot of really gorgeous collectibles (silver rounds, etc.) for just slightly over spot silver price (current commodities market price for 100 ounce ingots) because when you go to the coin/bullion shop to sell, they don't care what the Bradford Exchange or the Franklin Mint told you the value was when you bought it.

Junk silver can be bought in loose bags by face value (such as $100 face value, $500 face value, etc.), in tubes, or as loose coins. They are usually sold at a price some multiple of "face" value, or something like "10 times face."

Say you have a role of silver Washington quarters that has a face value of $10.

- $10 X .72 (approximate amount of silver in Troy ounces in one silver dollar) = 7.2 Troy ounces of silver

- 7.2 X $20 (approximate current spot price today) = $144 spot value, or 14.4 X face value

The spot price is the current market price at one of the markets trading in silver. This roll of coins is worth more than that because all silver and gold has a "premium" attached to it, which usually represents the cost of minting. The spot price is the per-ounce price for specially manufactured, certified, and stored 100-ounce ingots. All other silver usually costs more than that.

In this case, I would round up to 15 or 16 times face value and consider it a good deal if I could buy for that price.

You will have to go where the market takes you.

The second tier of this investment strategy is US Silver Eagles. These are beautiful one-ounce silver coins with a $1 face value. They have a high premium, usually at least $5 per coin, but they are easily recognizable and exchangeable. Note: Silver Eagles are one-ounce coins and are sold by the ounce. The formula for pre-1965 coins above does not apply.

Next are silver "rounds" and ingots. Silver rounds are privately minted silver coins. Ingots are virtually all privately minted. From private buyers, I have bought as low as spot price, and big bullion dealers will occasionally have promotions where you can buy for $.50 above spot (all plus shipping, of course).

My gold investments consist of US Gold Eagles and Chinese or Thai gold. US Gold Eagles come in 1 ounce, half ounce, quarter ounce, and 1/10th ounce. All have high premiums (as much as $50 a coin, no matter the weight) but again, they are easy to exchange. Thai/Chinese Gold comes in 22K (96%) and is easily bought and sold. The purity is high, and it can even be worn as jewelry. US bullion dealers know what it is and will buy it.

Where to Buy Gold and Silver?

In the early days (2000-2008), I bought a lot on eBay, but now that the prices of bullion are higher, there's been a proliferation of fakes. DYODD.

I've also bought from a local jewelry store. They accept old jewelry on trade from their customers, at well below spot price, but they don't like to sell it in their shop because it hurts their sales of new jewelry. I had a relationship with the owner, so I convinced him to sell me stuff out of his "junk box" at roughly spot price or slightly above. He made more money than he would if he sent it to the refiners, and I got some cool stuff.

For example, I once bought a twelve-setting antique silverware set, including serving spoons, salt and pepper shakers, and other paraphernalia, all in a nice walnut box for $1500, or maybe $50 over (the total) spot price. At the time, it would have easily cost $7500 if I had gone to

Nordstrom for something similar. I'm afraid to look at the price now for fear I'd get the urge to sell…

The best place for a newbie to start is a precious metals dealer, either a local or a reputable online dealer. The only online dealer I've ever bought from, and with whom I have been extremely satisfied, is the American Precious Metals Exchange (APMEX), which can be found at http://www.apmex.com.

Lastly, I'd like to make a note about food supplies.

With the modern-day "just in time" logistic system, there are really no more local warehouses of food to supply supermarkets. The vast majority of products in your local supermarket arrive "just in time" by long-haul trucks. That's another way of saying that all food in the USA is warehoused in trucks on the highway.

It is estimated that if the US diesel fuel supply was suddenly cut, as it might be after an accident or terrorist attack on a large refinery, that it would take about 48 hours for supermarket shelves to be empty. That's if nobody notices the trucks aren't rolling! If a panic starts, all bets are off.

For this reason, I try to keep about a year's supply of dried and preserved food available at home. I consider this part of my savings account, an "investment" I made when the commodities were at a relatively low price. (If there are food shortages, prices WILL rise!) This is really another form of "honest money," which is to say a commodity with stable value. I keep a good supply of water on hand as well as the means to purify more. After all, I can last a lot longer without food than I can without water.

We have at least one diesel car or truck at all times and a good number of cans of diesel fuel stored. Diesel stores much better and longer than gasoline. Other things like soap, laundry detergent, toilet paper, candles, batteries, etc. are all excellent items to have on hand in case of an emergency, either short or long term.

We refuel when the cars get to half a tank, so in case of a blizzard, hurricane, terrorist attack, or Viking Super Bowl victory celebration, (some of these are less likely than others in Minnesota), we will have a reserve. In short, we like to be ready for short- as well as long-term emergencies. We rotate the stock of consumables so nothing is really wasted.

My advice to you is to get out of debt, put away some silver and gold, get your financial house in order, get your physical house in order (prepare for emergency), but don't forget to live your life along the way. Being prepared for physical and financial disaster does not mean you have to be a "gloom and doomer." Continue to enjoy your life, feeling more secure in your ability to handle adversity.

Postscript

There is a scene in *The Matrix* where Neo, played by Keanu Reeves, is offered the choice between a red pill and a blue pill. Take the blue pill and go back to living your life the way you were, and you will forget we ever had this conversation. Take the red pill and learn how the world really works.

One of the members of our online forum goldismoney2.com has the forum nickname of "bluepillenvy" which made me laugh when I first saw it.

I have another friend who both curses and thanks me for giving him the red pill.

As we like to say in the forums, "Ignorance is like virginity. Once you lose it, you can never get it back!"

And finally, in the immortal words of Sir Robert Baden-Powell, founder of the Boy Scouts, "Be Prepared!"

Acknowledgements

I'd like to extend a special thank you to Jimmy Haagenson, who generously provided the images in Chapter 3. The currency pictured is from his eBay shop, which you can find at http://www.ebay.com/usr/templar1a. You can also find his book *Templar Secrets* on Amazon. Thanks, Jimmy!

Thank You

Thank you so much for reading this short primer on honest money. If it has helped you view money in a different way, then I am heart-warmed to know that it has served its purpose.

Before I buy a book online, I always read the reviews written by people who have already read it. The reviews weigh heavily in my decision to buy or not. Please take a few moments to let other readers know what you think about *Honest Money*.

I would also like to offer you a free gift in exchange for signing up for my newsletter. *Once Upon a Time: A Financial Fable* is an historical satire about the fictional "Freedomlovers" who flee their island kingdom for liberty and opportunity but find themselves trapped by a system they don't understand. If you liked *Honest Money*, I'm sure you'll enjoy *Once Upon a Time*. It's yours, free, just for signing up for my newsletter!

The sign-up page is at http://www.dailydiatribe.net/hm

You have my word I will never sell or share your e-mail address, nor will I bombard you with annoying advertisements. Of course, you can easily and conveniently unsubscribe any time by simply clicking on the "unsubscribe" button, which will be present in every newsletter.

For news about upcoming books, such as *When All Else Fails*, about how failing to follow the Constitution has caused most of the problems in the USA, and *Sex, Lies, & Carbohydrates, How I Accidentally Lost 30 Pounds*, you can also visit my website at:

http://www.dailydiatribe.net

Or the Daily Diatribe Facebook page at:

https://www.facebook.com/pages/Daily-Diatribe/494566093924000

Warm regards,

Carl

*It is well enough that
people of the nation do not
understand our banking
and monetary system, for if
they did, I believe there
would be a revolution
before tomorrow morning.*

—Henry Ford,
Founder of the Ford Motor Company